AN ARRANGED MARRIAGE

WISHFUL OR FORCEFUL

RISHABH SRIVASTAVA

One Day,

Someone Told Me To Suggest Her A Book So that She Could Read and Include Book Reading Into Her Daily Habit. I Thought Of Gifting Her This Book as A Surprise.

Yes, This One is Dedicated To You.

Along Side,

My Family, Everyone Who Knows Me, Friends, Enemies. This One's For You.

Contents

Preface   *vii*

Controversy

  1. No To Arrange Marriages   7

  2. Breaking Stereotype   13

  3. Society Rules   26

  4. Being Judge-mental   31

  5. Ego Or Self Respect   35

  6. Dowry   38

  7. Violence   46

  8. Love And Love   49

  9. Settlements   52

  10. Yes To Love   58

Preface

I've Seen Many Heart Broken People Who Sacrificed Their Love Just Because of Society Rules, Tradition, Religion Boundation. Today Many People are Sacrificing Their Love and Getting Married Into Arranged Form Of Love Just because they are not able to coupe up the things.

In Today's Century Where Being Happy Should be The first Preference Of the People In that era People are Following The Custom Of Arranged Marriage That too With So much of Illogical Things and Stupidity. In This Book I'll Just Try to pitch My Idea Regarding Arranged Marriage and Try to show What I Feel Wrong About it.

Controversy

This is my first book, I have never tried such things before but what I think is this book is going to be really Controversial cause it will speak the truth and *"Truth always Carries Controversies"*.

This book will not create controversy in the society or in the so called "SAMAAJ", Neither it will create Controversy between 4 most Educated person in the entire Universe whom we don't know personally but heard of them many times in our society by our parents, relative and everyone. Those 4 educated Man are probably known as *"4 log" (now maybe some pseudo feminist might say why 4 men not women)* Rather it will create controversy not only in my family but in the family of everyone who think love marriages are biggest sin on the planet.

The people who think Love marriages are sin should check today's Newspaper if you still didn't get it then you should probably read your Holy Scriptures and point out the line where its written that being happy with some-one through entire life is a sin rather living with Hate, Anger, Depression and with a false Ego.

It is totally shocking that In India Where people always worship Lord Krishna along with his soulmate Radha. People Never Pronounce Krishna's Name Alone We Always say *"Radhekrishna". We Never ever Put a "-" (Dash) Between RadheKrishna Because we believe in their*

Togetherness in That Country the mentality of people is like *"WO HAMARI BIRADARI KI NAHI HAI \ WO HAMARI HAISIYAT KI NAHI HAI"*.

(she is not among our caste \ status).

Dude What is this behaviour?

Are you comedy me?

Are you talking about your caste your status?

What does it need to do with Someone's happiness?

If Status, Caste, Religion, Money is essential for our Happiness then you should think twice that you are the most depressed man in the entire universe because there is someone more Wealthy then you, At upper caste then you or more Religious then you.

There Are Many People Whom I know personally, Supports Love Marriages By saying *"Ab Bacche logo ko hi rehna hai wo khush to ham khush"* but when some baccha does a love marriage they don't even talk with them neither with their partner. I have Just One Question

Why Do We Hate someone Who does Love marriage?

Why Do We Prefer Our Ego over someone's Happiness?

Not just these two questions, You see in our society, family or even within ourselves you will find not two nor three but Thousands and Thousands of such questions.

The Problem doesn't lies in the society nor in the people of the society but in oneself. You might disagree with this statement but just assume if you are correct and everyone is wrong,

Is everything sorted from your side?

Do you stand against these people, stereotype, Idea these people have regarding arrange marriages?

Just Because they didn't do as we expected them to do or else. If you know such people please try to make them clear all the hate regarding someone and make them talk over cell phone and clear the hate issues and start a new bond among them.

In This world where We Prefer 'Vasudeva kutumbakam", (The World is our Family) On that planet where people believe that we may grow much faster and Live much Happier by Collaborating and And sharing our joy or sorrow With someone, But sometime we also Try to deal with Independence by saying "I'll Do it alone"

In Class 8 we have studied A Chapter in Mathematics, Work and time.

And in that chapter there was a Sub-Topic known as "Men, Days and work."

You Might be Familiar with the General Question That

If a Single man Can built a wall in 10 days then how much time will it take to build the same wall by 5 Men?

Now just Use a little common sense and answer the Question in just a simple Language, Will 5 men take less time or a man will take less time?

Obviously 5 Men will take much less time.

The Only Chapter Of Mathematics that we can use in general day to day life problems whether its Dealing with our Ego, Happiness, Sorrow or Misery.

Yes I Totally Agree that You might be able to do it by your own or you might not be able to do it by your own but The fact is It will take more time and in today's world where people already are running out of time. We are wasting this precious gift just for our ego to build that wall Alone.

Leave It, Use 5 Men or more but Try to save Time, Share Happiness, not Ego or self Attribution.

On the other Day I was Just Scrolling some Blogs and Found a very Beautiful Story By Shukanya Dutta.

Once upon a time there was an island, where all the feelings lived together, One day there was a storm in the sea and the island was about to drown. Every feeling was scared but love made a boat to escape. Every feeling borrowed the boat. One feeling was left. Love got down to see who it was. It was Ego. Love tried and tried but Ego don't move. Everyone asked love to leave but love was meant to love, it remained with ego. All the other feelings left alive but love died because of ego.

This simple and amazing story clearly helps us to differentiate between love and ego.. Love and ego have certain proportions in our life. When they are balancing to each other nothing worse happens, but when ego's effect is too much than love A drastic Change happens in one's life, then it becomes really tough to Think about "U" than "I"..."I" becomes so important that love is lost for forever...Someone said "ego is like a dust in the eyes....without cleaning this you can't see anything clearly...so skip the "e" and let it "go"!

But In the case of Love Marriage the Boat is Different, The Feelings are different and Ego is Not Of the lovers but of the society.

And in the Ego of society Love Always Drowns and Ego Always Floats.

So From Now I'm Handling My Pen's Control To the society.

I'm Not Gonna Write Something Extra But Just Portray The Exact Replica Of Our Society So if you think this book is telling something wrong or unusual just see in our society You will find that its much more devastating then its written on this book.

CHAPTER ONE

No To Arrange Marriages

Hold On Hold On,

Let me Clear One thing I am not completely against Arrange Marriage but their are many flaws in our society regarding Arrange marriage, One of the main flaw which I find it a product of human 'keen' Mindset. We Always say "Kyuki Saas bhi kabhi bahu thi" (Probably watch it also) but is it so?

Do we Really mean it?

Do we really follow it?

Or we just use it as Weapon while in a serious situation during a debate.

When we go to select a daughter-in-law we tend to test her more then we test some mobile phones while buying it.

We shoot some serious Questions at her with most dangerous weapon humanity has ever got. More Dangerous then Nuclear Weapon, Atom Bomb or a Supersonic weapon that can destroy the earth in one blow

Yes You Guessed it right

'A human tongue'

Its more dangerous because in a nuclear weapon people die with the wounds but with a human tongue People live with the wound.

And a wounded human is more dangerous than a wounded lion.

By the way lets get back to the topic

We shoot some serious questions like

- Do you Know how to Cook?
- Do you know All household works?
- Sing Something
- Play Any Musical Instrument
- Any Previous Relationship?
- Any Affairs ? Etc etc

Not just With Ladies people ask These Silly Questions with Men too.

How Much Do you earn?

Do You Smoke?

Any Previous Relationship? Etc

I am having just one question with the society

Does these silly questions make their bonds stronger and increase their love?

But the tables have turned and karma has showed his power

When its time for our Own daughter We tell her not to smile much, not to speak much, behave properly etc.

The Family where an unmarried daughter lives behaves on just one principal

"Bas Kaise Kaise Iski Shadi Ho Jaye".

Kaise Kaise?

Are you serious?

She is your daughter, you have given Birth to her you haven't rented her as your apartment she is your own daughter.

- You have taught her
- you have Given her What ever she wanted

- You Both have shared some beautiful moments of joy
- You Both have cried during family problems
- You have protected her from bad guys

Now you are pushing her into the darker swamp of Arrange Marriage where you have met your son-in-law just a month back or maybe 2 months back

How come you know that he is a nice guy?

Maybe he is faking himself, Its easy to fake now-a-days that to in 21st Century. Where people are Professionally faking smiles and lifestyles on social media he can do it to?

Its not a bigger deal.

6 Out of 10 Couples are not really Satisfied with their Partner.

Kindly don't get another meaning of satisfied. I am not saying happy because in arrange marriage searching happiness is just like searching needle in a hay. What is a reason of being so?

Just because some elder member of the family said "hum apne baccho ke liye bura thodi sochenge"

Their is a possibility that You might not think bad about your child but What is the possibility that you will think best for your child?

Once in a billion unlike Dr Strange said to iron man while Fighting Thanos?

Yes that might be elders are just like Dr Strange who are searching for possibilities to choose the best son-in-law for his daughter but let me tell you one thing but promise me you won't laugh at this.

The Criteria for choosing a great son-in-law is

- Having enough cash
- Must have his own house
- Family must be nice
- He Should not smoke or drink

But where is the fucking proof that he will keep your daughter safe and keep on loving through out his life and will not have extra marital affairs after marriage too?

Dear Please Choose a Loving Partner for your Daughter not a Atm machine and with due respect I want to say please change the criteria for choosing a son in law you are not choosing a candidate for your corporation or a manager for your accounting firm you are choosing a perfect son in law for your Princess.

Think Wisely Think Lovingly.

People Always Say that "He The Almighty, who makes them united"

They Why Do people Inter Fear Them with their Rituals, Stupid Thoughts and Their Judging Skills.

Are they Challenging The Choice of Their Almighty?

Are They Trying to Change His decision?

What I Personally Feel today may Let your Believe system to be hurt a bit because we have been piling these traditions for so long that we have forgotten to question it.

And You all might agree on the Thought that "Things Needs To be changed over time, If Not it becomes A So called daily Routine, Without any meaning.

There Were A Bunch of Monkeys Living in the Zoo some Where In Africa.

One Day a Monkey Named Zuffu Was Sitting On the Top of his Chambers. The surrounding was so beautiful and the zoo looked Heavenly from the top and then suddenly due to some Electrical Damage The Pipe on which Zuffu was sitting Carried a High Voltage current and Zuffu Died.

Since Then His Families and Friends Living in the same Chambers Ordered Everyone Not to Touch that Pipe Because It is Electrically Active and From then No one questioned or Touched That Pipe.

Although It was Just a Co-Incidence that Zuffu Died, Since then All monkeys were so fond that they didn't Even looked at that pipe because they thought that it would harm them.

And then Ages Passed and The upcoming Generations Of monkeys Changed the Prospective From that Pipe is electrically Active to its Harmful, God Punishes us, Or some Generations Even told That they are In the hands of Black Magic who so ever touches it need to be punished

From Then No one ever Asked but Simply Obeyed the order From Their Elders that "Don't Touch The Pipe"

So You see The Prospective of monkeys changed over time and they Stopped Questioning About why we should not climb on the top, Rather they are missing the beautiful View of the zoo from the top.

Darwin Once Said We Are born From Monkeys, This Story Fits Perfect if we follow darwin's Theory.

We Are just like monkeys Missing the Top View and the beautiful nature just by following the tradition Without Questioning.

Someone Needs to Challenge it and Make a Front mark for Everyone so that they may Get a Beautiful view of life.

Traditions and Rituals Needs to Be Understood by the upcoming generations as clear as many doubt as it could be rather then simply saying "it needs to be Followed"

Traditions are made for people, People are not Made For Traditions.

Their are So much Unasked Tradition in Arrange Marriages that People are Following Them at Very High Speed by sacrificing the Happiness, Peace and Ruining a beautiful gift From God

That's "LIFE"

CHAPTER TWO

BREAKING STEREOTYPE

Do You Know What is fixed in the common belief system Of Indian Society?

Can You Guess What Is The First Question They Ask While In The Arrange Marriage?

Do You Know To get A love Marriage Its Really Lucky In India Because Your Love Needs to Pass Through Several Filters. Dude I'm Not Kidding Your Love Needs To Pass Through

- Same Nationality Filter
- Same Religion Filter
- Same Caste and Creed Filter
- Your Male Partner Needs To be Elder
- Female Partner Must Be Approved By EMF Federation Of India(Every Member Of The Family Federation of India)
- A Maanglik(Most Important Filter)

Congratulations! If You Have Successfully Passed All The Exams Created By EMF Federation Of India And Now

You are Thinking that " Ab To Hamari Shadi ho hi jayegi Ab Kon Rokega"

Then You are Absolutely Wrong And then Suddenly An Old Uncle Will Appear According to whom If Their is a love Marriage In A family Then Its a Lost of Respect and Dignity Of the Family Members (I Am Not Sure What Respect And Dignity They Are Talking About That Is above Happiness).

They Generally use this weapon on the opening day of arrange marriage but in love marriage The case is different. They use it when they know that it is impossible to win this War Of Dignity So they will reach the upper men of Dictatorship Probably the Parents of partners And Tell them Very Smoothly "Kundali Match ho rahi?"

And Generally Modern Day Partners Are not prepared for this weapon so either they are Broke or they Broken Living. In Both Cases They Are No Longer A Part of Happily Living Minorities In This Only Universe.

Let Me Tell You A Funny Irony In My Family:-

One Among The 4 Most Educated Men In Society lives in my Relations

Once When I Crossed My Limit And Asked A logical Questions to Elders In My Family Then Suddenly That Relative Popped Out by Wearing Sanskaar To his forehead and he suddenly told me "The Ideal Age For Marriage is 22 years" I too got Married At very young maybe The Motive behind his sentence was "If I am trapped then how could you enjoy life" But you know what is the irony behind this ?

He Is a Die Hard Fan of salmaan khan.

"Are Maine Kaha Hypocrisy ki bhi seema hoti hai."

I Would like to write 4 Lines From One Of My Favourite Song,

Na Umr Ki Seema Ho, Na Janm Ka Ho Bandhan

Jab Pyaar Kare Koi, To Dekhe Keval Man

{If You are singing not reading these lines than you have a good taste in music} These 4 Lines are enough to break each and every Stereotype On this planet but its impossible for a human to understand the meaning of the words given by legends that's why people sometimes missunderstands Krishna, Ram or even Allah. You see Peter Dinklage commonly known as Tyrion Lannister From Game of thrones Web show. He is just 1.35 Meters Roughly around 4'5 Inches But The kind of Talent That Guy Has, He is the Power House Of the Talent as well as in breaking the stereotype. He has been happily married to Erica Schmidt Who is 1.68 meters roughly around 5'6Feet. The Question Is Fair enough will society accept it? Whether you see When Priyanka Chopra and Nick Jonas Got married and it was a national debate I Was Shocked that how could media couldn't Find 2 Men And make them fight on a national television Which often they like now a days where national security is our top most priority in that era how could A Indian Girl be Married to a foreigner that too 10 years younger? Until She Is Mentally Unstable or People Also Said and Tweeted that Its Not Appropriate But Let me ask a straight question to all them Who are we to ask those questions?

We Haven't Known Her Personally Nor she is interested in knowing these kind of people but I would like to Salute Her for breaking the stereotype And Also Like to congratulate her family for listening to her daughter For her happiness rather than Relatives. Not Only These Their are Plenty of Examples Present in our society that breaks or unfollows our Stereotypes. What I think is Some People are very good at making a set of rules Nor For them but for Someone Else, Which we will talk in Chapter 3 in Detail.

Now We Will Talk about the filters which you need to pass in a EMF Federation Each Filters plays an important role on your impression in front of the board Panels that are present in front of you till you are happily married or peacefully dead.

- SAME NATIONALITY FILTER

Let Me Revise your General Knowledge Their are 195 Countries On this planet Earth and to be happily married you need to Love someone From Same Country. You Know What is The Probability For that? But Before That Let Me Tell You Something The Current Population on the world on 10 January 2022 at 10:10PM was 7,917,373,269 people. I'm Sure You Haven't Read The Number But now You Could Easily Guess What is the Probability Of Finding that one person who will change your life but let me Throw a Molly. You Kindly increase the probability because that one person must be From Your Country Too And If You Still think its easy then For Your Kind Information Let Me Remind You that there are 6 More Tests That You have to pass To get a happy and charming partner. There Are People who are breaking these kind of rules set by society. Prity Zinta, Karishma Kapoor are set of front benchers who have done it already whom people admired the most. People Questioned them Also. People also Commented on them But they remained Strong And believed in their loved one. I Know Being from the same country and fell in love feels different but that does not mean that we curb the ways to spread our love All over the world. Love Is All About Opening the path towards happiness and caring but the stereotypes are limiting it down. I Assume that you have read the story about a wolf who wore the lions costume and fooled everybody out there but when the truth was revealed Everyone took the hell shit out of it. In Arrange Marriage This Story Remains Same But The Result is different When partner tend to pretend that they are modern and western by wearing Tuxedo Suits and Formals but dear are you also modern from inside? Your Thinking, Ideas, Mentality does it match with the western tradition or its just a story of a wolf wearing Lion's Skins. As I told you the Result is little different When The other partner finds out that western was just like the lions costume from inside he is just a wolf. Nobody in the fucking universe take the shit out of the wolf people just say To that Female "Ab To Shadi Ho Gayi Kya Kar Sakte hai?"

Divorce Kar Sakte hai?

Divorce, Pagal Ho Jamana Kya Kahega?

Is Society More Important or Happiness?

Happiness(Outside) {Society(Inside)}.

You Might Laugh at This or may feel bad About the society but let me tell you a harsh reality Your Family Is also a part that Society and sometime you might also be a part of this. Just ask yourself a Question? Am I Worth Faking?

What if The Same Thing Happens With Me?

What Will Happen If i am on the other side of the goal? To Change the society and remove all the filters from the arrange marriage you just need to ask yourself a question and if you are elder member of the family you need to ask question to everyone. Change The filters regarding Nationality caste creed and other aspects to make arrange marriages a better place after getting married or spending nearly 20-30 years with your partner. Now Lets Talk about the second filter and probably most dangerous one I'll Not go into much deep because that might land me in a big trouble Because in the matter of religion people always taught us not to question, Don't Ask Illogical question God Might Become angry. Dude Does your father Ever Slapped you or Punished you for Asking question?

No matter how foolish it might be. And Secondly If God doesn't want us to Ask questions on him then never ever he will give us that upper part of the Head i.e brain but What can we do Our Luck is not as strong as Politicians.

- Same Religion Filter

Let Me Ask to the young blood of our nation, to the generations who are fighting for their Religion without Knowing what Exactly is Religion?

What Is Religion?

Someone Who has Read all the holy scriptures all the holy Book might Fire some Sanskrit Sloke which no one knows the meaning neither I nor they.

I know Just A Four Liners of saint Kabir which perfectly fits on today's People.

Pothi Padh Padh Jag Mua, Pandit Bacha Na Koi
Dhai Akhar Prem Ka, Padhe So Pandit Hoe

I Know nothing about Religion but one thing I know for sure that Religion is just a way of living.

Either you read Quran. Geeta, Guru Granth Sahib or Bible that only thing religion Teaches us is To love and serve the Mankind. I Think I should Dug A little Bit deep inside this topic because Its one Along my zone. There are plenty of thoughts and Emotions I need to Discuss with you guys.

Today is 14th Feb 2022 The day of love.

People Misinterpreted This day And started a propaganda That its only made for lovers and couples its not like This. Its a Day of Love whether Parents, Nation, Partner or anyone You Wish to thank and confront about your love and your caring But back in the morning I watched a video of some Group of people beating a young couple Because they were sitting in the park while holding hands.

Where Are We Heading as a nation?

And the reason people give after Boycotting And beating Couples on Valentine Day is that Its A western Culture We Would not let our young generation influence by the Western Culture.

Dude

- Have You Ever Wondered Why Our Cars Have Steering Wheels on the Right Side Of the Car?
- Have You Ever Wondered Why Walk Along Left Side Of the road?

Because Britishers Influenced us And in British Empire People Walked from Left and Drove their Vehicles From Right. Britishers Even Ruled Americans but when they left Americans Denied their Influence And Shifted everything opposite that is the basic reason they walk from right and drive from left.

Not Just these two reasons Their are plenty of reasons at which We are influenced from British.

Fun Fact:-

Do You Know that Indian Constitution Had Been Summed up From constitutions of 10 Countries. Ever Wondered Which Could Be The First Country?

Its United Kingdom

Nothing Wrong in it that's How Humanity and human works Taking good from others and Removing bad.

Religion in Marriage is as similar as Lies In Politics.
(Whether you agree or not it exist)

Today Inter Cast Marriages have been made More Complicated due to some political agenda. Some People Call It Love Jihad Or even may call them by different Name but the draw back is same You Seperate the Lovers. You Can Not Apart the Love not you nor you boss not even the supreme Leader(Not Talking About God. He Knows What Love is).

I've Heard People Saying "Our Families Won't Agree", "Society Won't Accept Inter Cast Marriage."And Crying Over Phones while doing the last call, hearing their partner's Voice Last time, Every Promise Vanished Every Dream they saw went Thousands feet below the ground ever Wondered Why this all Happen Just Because we are bounded by the boundaries of religion.

God Never Created Religion He Can't be that much hard hearten.

When You Will Read Hindu Holy Scripture "Shri Mat Bhagwat Geeta" Lord Krishna Stated Love Plenty of time but he never stated Religion at once.He Never stated about Hindu Word Once in entire Bhagwat Geeta, Yes I agree that He Mentioned Sanatan Dharm and Hinduism follows Sanatan Dharm but Hinduism is a totally different word then Sanatan Dharma.

There is a great difference between a religion and a dharma. A religion is something that is founded by someone. A religion is where a large group of people share a common symbol, a common religious text, a common GOD and a common founder. A religion is something that consists of a group of followers who earlier followed a different faith but now are following a certain faith that they now believe in. A religion is one which was founded by a religious movement. A religion has a date of origin. A religion is a set of belief systems.

Dharma on the other hand is more of a way of living or a way of life followed since antiquity, i.e., since the start of civilisation. Dharma was a kind of education or knowledge imparted to a person to lead a life in a certain way. Dharma is also sometimes considered as a complete and continuous education. Dharma is based on the principle of truth. Dharma is based on various stages that a man passes through in his lifetime, i.e., birth, childhood, youth, old age and death. Dharma is the truth or Dharma is the righteousness. If Karma is the righteous action, Dharma is the righteous decision. Dharma is not preached. Dharma is learnt, followed and practised. Dharma is the role you play.

The Dharma that was practiced in the ancient times has a multitude of difference than what is practised at the present time. Now Dharma has become a synonym with the religion. A religion is not a Dharma.

Well In Simple Words Religion has its origin in the west, by the followers of Abraham. Dharma has its origin India. In religion we have single God, a Prophet or savior and a holy book which alone is the way of liberation, whereas in dharma we have **many ways and all the ways leads to same God.**

People Should accept human being as he is and understand his feelings his love according to his own prospective rather then burdening them with Religion Caste Creed and other Things.

- Same Caste and creed

You Will be Shocked to know that in India there are 3000+ Casts and more then 25000 Sub-Casts and to find a perfect partner who fits in that 3000 casts filter and then also get selected in rest 25000 sub casts.

This Much Criteria is Required to get a love marriage where both society and family members lives together and happily.

Is it not better to be unmarried and save all our powers that would have been lost in searching a perfect bride and use all that in our roadies audition?

People Have Strange Logics in telling why their Caste is more Educated and Upper Class. Some People Also use their Sixth Sense in Proving that their Caste is More Superior and Dominating in this society{ Except General One's A Huge Thanks To Reservation}.

The Second Most Ignored Thing in India Is Love Marriage, People of General caste Still Remains the First. During Election Rallies Of Politicians and Speeches Always Revolves around 1000 Crore Funds Regarding Poor and some Great Projects for Rich once but where is Middle class or lower Middle Class?

We Have Been One's Spending more On Education, We are the one Spending More on Health(and still not getting properly), We are the one paying huge taxes yet we are the one those are most ignored too.

People Of Middle Class Is Something like Self Respect While Messaging your Crush, They are Like Cardamom In Briyani Or even when you zoom in and see them closer you will be shocked to find that they are the one's who are present like a housefly in the tea of Annual Budget on Our Country. Nothing Much Just Thrown Outside and served to the Poor and the Rich.

Female Partner Must Be Approved By EMF Federation Of India(Every Member Of The Family Federation of India)

Let Me Share My Personal Story,

When They Reached My Mother For The Wedding proposal(Obviously People From My Father Side), As Mentioned In my Older Conversations They asked silly Questions Like

Do you know to play Two Headed Hand Drum Popularly Known As Dholak In Northern Areas of India.

Is Their anything or anyway this question is related to marriage?

You Might Think This Is Just a simple Story They Might Have asked just casually but you are not thinking About the backside Of the story.

Obviously They have said this Question Because while in family gathering in Indian Northern areas Playing Dholak Represents A good Musical skills that might uplifts the Respect of family whom the candidate represents but but

What If My Mother Didn't Know to Play Dholak at that time?

Then Its not just A Matter of skill, People Will Suddenly Put Fingers on The Upbringing Of the child. It may or may not by The People Of my Fathers Side But also It Goes Into The Mentality of the Society that she is not able to play two headed side drum. She Might be Taking care of her Family in the best possible ways but while in public or in family gatherings she might feel little uncomfortable or under-confident in the Beginning Of her Second Journey.

You Might Say that It was A Mentality of people in older days but now it has changed a lot but Instead of asking about dholak Modern Society has Replaced This Question by Asking Have you were in any relationship before?

This Is Indirect Version Of Asking Are You Virgin?

Now after this statement you might think that "What's Wrong in Asking this Question"

I Say Their is Nothing Wrong in it if you are choosing a girl as a wife for your Son and as your daughter in law then You must also stick to the fact that You also need to ask your son about previous Relationships.

In India Where Mothers Quote their son by saying " You Are too Smart You can get any girl easily"

In The Era of this Quote also mothers tell their daughter not to fall for anyone.

"Irony Hori Bohot Bhayankar, Irony ke hai gazab najare."

Sometimes I think :-

- Who Started these kind of Rituals?
- Who Followed These Rituals?
- Why We are caring it on our shoulders?
- Is It Necessary?

And only logical Answer i could Think of is, Only the people who care much about their respect among Four Most uneducated men in the society(As mentioned several times) Follow this kind of illogical Unsymmetrical Act.

You might agree on the fact that only people that have limited wealth and respect care more for them rather then owing Happiness to someone.

Lets Suppose,

I Give you A Magical pot and every time you give it to somebody it doubles.

One for you and for someone you have given.

Will you be happy in just doing one double?

Or will you give it to every damn person who crosses your way?

Happiness and Love are The magical pot That Doubles when you pass it.Just Smile to a random Person While being in stress and boom the magical pot doubles itself, He Smiled Back.

25

CHAPTER THREE

SOCIETY RULES

People Always Misunderstand the saying, Every War since the existence of the universe has happened because of females but the point they are misleading is, When a woman can end an entire dynasty without picking up the weapon then what will happen when she will pick the weapon.

I am very much Impressed by the Points Hindu Shastra has Told and expressed their thoughts about woman. According To Hindu Shastra, Only One thing that is Superior to God That is Women.

Lord Krishna While Reciting Mahabharata to Arjuna Told Him That:

Yatra Naristu Pujyate, Ramane Tatra Devta
Yatretastu na Pujyate Sarvasatraphala Kriya

Where Women are honoured, divinity blossoms there, and where ever women are dishonoured, all action no matter how noble it may be, remains unfruitful.

What We Have Done, We have captured the women into the Chains of rules, It Seems We Have Forgotten The Rudra Avatar of a women who was so unstoppable that Even the Gods Were Not Able to stop them.

They Were Fearing to Face The Rudra avatar of a women so they send Lord Shiva to do so And what are we doing? We Have Made a Certain set of rule for a female.

We have completely Forgotten that Woman who makes the rules, Leads Her Family into Happy way.

Even If you Turned up the history books, you might See several Injustices happened to a women including "Sati Pratha", "Breast Tax Revolt", Or even "Early Child Marriages"

But Even after Hundreds and Thousands of years Later the things have not Gone better.

Today Woman Face Gender Abuse, Rape Threat and Dependence.

By Dependence I don't mean They are not free or can not do Any Thing by their own, The only thing is that They need to ask permission from someone.

In Arrange Marriage that rules plays a vital role in Bringing an idle daughter-in-law.

Whether Its About Dressing Sense, To Behave Properly, Not to Laugh Loudly, Not to walk in a manly way, Not to Argue Elders.

First of all I totally disagree by the logic that younger One should not argue with elder nor Should question their decisions.

I Mean Its not true that Elders are Always Right or younger one are always wrong its about the logic or the Stage at which we deal with the problem, If A Younger Being is giving some Advice Regarding Any Situation Of Life You Need to Listen Through it and Tell him about the consequences Of his Idea. This Will Empower The Child To Focus and Think Of something Better and will also increase their Problem solving skills.

The Same Problem Lies In The Married Life Also, The Dominating Partner Never Listens To The Other Partner Whether He is a male partner or a female partner. In Arrange Marriage We Have To Follow A set of rules so it takes a lot of time to mix up with our environment and live comfortably because until we live comfortably we Can not live peacefully.

You Need to dress Properly

You Need To Behave Properly

You Need To Talk Properly

You Need to Walk Properly

and Many More.

Do We Teach These Things to our Daughter?

Or Even Son?

If We Don't Follow our own Rules then how we can Make Someone follow it(Until We are a Politician).

You Will Find Nearly 99.99 Percent of Indian Families saying "Ye To Hamari Beti Jaisi Hai","She Seems like my own Daughter".

But Actually How many Families Literally Stand Upon Their Words?

Like Around 5%

So You See That's Where The Trouble Begin, That Percentage That Damn Percentage.

Out Of 99 Women Only 5 are lucky enough to be treated as Daughter in their Second home. Rest Remained Silent Throughout their Lives or became rebellious and that's where Destruction of the family starts.

Why are making such a double headed rules for Daughter in Law?

A Set Of Different Rules for Daughter and Daughter in Law?

It was never answered even in 1922 nor it will be answered now, the only thing that has changed is After Marriage Happiness Index has been fallen Deeply.

You Will Find many Husband Wife jokes on social Media And people Find it funny also But In Every Case They Show Husband as a victim and wife as a dominator but is it so?

Men Can laugh and Share their Injustice and the chains of rules by the society in a manner of sarcasm but Woman can not.

The Society will Taunt her Just Because They are made for it,

They are Made For the Rules that Society Has Made To Limit Their Energies.

Have You Watched A Marval Movie Named "Thor-Ragnarok"

Its One of my Favourite Scene as Follows

Thor: I'm Thor, Son of Odin.

Hela: Really? You Don't Look Like Him?

Loki: Perhaps We can Come to An Arrangement

Hela: You Sound Like Him, Kneel

Loki: Beg Your Pardon?

Hela: Kneel, Before Your Queen

Thor: I don't Think so

And then Thor Throws His Hammer Towards Hela and She Stops It Single Handedly.

Thor: Its Not Possible

Hela: Darling, You Have No Idea What's Possible

(and then She Destroys his hammer)

That hammer Could be A set of rules that Society Creates for a woman and thor could be a Society

When Woman Who knows her Worth Can be As Dangerous as Hela and she can Break All set of Hammers

Single Handedly with Just a Smile.
At Last "Darling You Have No Idea What's Possible"

CHAPTER FOUR

BEING JUDGE-MENTAL

India now has almost**4 crore** pending cases spanning the Supreme Court, various high courts and the numerous district and subordinate courts, according to written replies submitted by the Ministry of Law and Justice in Parliament. That compares with 3.65 crore total pending cases in India as of Feb. 1, 2020.

India now has almost 1273289 Lawyers in Each Court whether Supreme Court, High Court or even District Courts and approximately but you will to be shocked to know that India Has more Judges then Lawyers.

Now You Might be thinking what rubbish I'm Talking, No Really India has Enormous number of Judges But the only difference is that they don't sit inside the Court as they Are Imposters among Us.

They Might be found On Chai Ki Tapri, Restaurants or even at your own Blood, and Discussing about Married life or even your career and Slowly they pour sweet poison Inside Elder members of the family and at last they say "Humko Kya karna hai", "What we have to do"

(Jab Tumko Kuch Karna hi nahi tha to zeher Ghola hi kyu, Apshabd)

In Our Country we are brought up in such a way that we start trusting people easily. We Trust Strangers Rather Then Someone Our Close And this gives Birth to a New Kind of Disease Known as Trusting issue.

When You Trust Strangers or anyone outside the family you start loosing trust of your family members. According to you what ever family will say or how well the idea is you will find a mistake and you will wait for the verification from that 3rd Person. This Also Spoils Family Relationships and the environment of the house.

Well In Arrange Marriage Showing how well daughter-in-law has been arrived to our house is the first Priority of the Indian Elders and to be showcased about their decision of not letting their Child to be married by the girl of his own choice (Maybe of different religion or caste) and be proud of this.

I'm Not saying all of them are like this but when you will move to Ruler Areas This problem seems quite serious, and some people are absolutely unaware about the mental pressure and stress it is giving to married couple, not only telling about Male Members but also the female has been suppressed more then ever.

Have you ever thought that this could ruin someone life or even the happiness of the family not the marriage not the people but the bullshit decision you are proud of.

Elders often say about choosing the finest Bride or groom for their child but as i told only 5 out of 99 are lucky enough to be chosen by a perfect partner are rest suffer throughout their lives. They Also Have A famous Dialogue Coming from 1560 that" Why we will think Bad for our child."

I am not saying that you are thinking bad for your child but have you ever Heard the story of an innocent child?

Well Their was a Child of age 5 years (who lived in everyone of us) he went on a holiday to a lake with family and as soon as he saw fish swimming in a pond he jumped and caught the fish and made his way out.

Now you may be thinking that how foolish, Fishes live in pond that child has killed it.

But What if i told you that child was not thinking bad about the fish he just took it out because he thought it was drowning.

Their is no Difference Between an Elder trying to be good to his child(In Terms of searching a partner) and an innocent boy taking fish out of the pond,

Both Never thought bad.

Your Son is not a child any more he is mature enough to decide whom he gonna married. He Just Need Your support to fight the 3rd person living outside what if you are the 3rd Person. Have You Ever thought about it?

How much mental pressure Youths are getting today?

- About Career
- Family
- Partner
- Job
- Money

And many more things.

So Just One thing Listen to your heart and to your family rather then listening to some dumb third person.

Or Else you will see Everything is falling apart and burning in front of your eyes and you could not do anything because you followed the 3rd person.

Suddenly a Person Behind Your Back Starts Laughing
Yes Its A 3rd Person.

CHAPTER FIVE

EGO OR SELF RESPECT

Ego is a type of human behaviour in which a person exclusively thinks and cares about himself. They don't think anyone is better than them, and they're always striving to outdo each other.

On the other hand

Self-respect is defined as the recognition of one's own worth and value. People that have self-respect regard themselves while also valuing others. They are not only concerned with their own desires and needs, but also with those of others. They respect but do not idolize themselves.

People today are very much confused between Self-Respect and Ego.

I Know Its Very Much Confusing But we need to draw a thin line between these or else everyone will fall apart as sand in a fist.

In People Day To Day Life Ego Plays A Very Vital role.

You are Going somewhere somebody scratched your vehicle your ego comes into action , Somebody Abused you Your Ego Mode Is activated.

We Humans Just need one line to cross all the anger limits and that line is

"How Could He?"

And Perhaps unlike him You Do The Same.

Is their any difference between the people who did this and you?

If He Abuses I'll Also Abuse'

if He Scratches my car I'll also do the same'

Someone Correctly said, "If You Kill a Murderer For His Murder then the Number Of Murderer in this world remains the same."

There Was a famous king who has won every war he fought. Once he got to know that his Old Friend who was very Poor and didn't have Clothes to wear , food to eat or even Place to live.

So The King thought to invite him at his place and make him realise that today "where are you and what i am" sort of thing(First Stage Of Destruction).

The Old Friend who was Poor arrived after months of walking because he didn't have any vehicle. On the Day On his Arrival the king decided to decorate the whole city by flowers and Candles with beautiful scents and girls dancing, Wines and every possible Way to show his richness.

It Took Almost two Months to king to prepare all these arrangement and it looked second space to heaven.

When The Old Friend Reached outside the palace the king was standing with all his enforcement, Golds Silver to Gift his old friend whom he met after several years. He Suddenly noticed Friend's Leg was poured into the mud till knees and the king was shocked, In His area people were suffering from starvation rain didn't happened since months.

When The King and his guards Escorted His Old Friend towards his Room, The Expensive Carpet was Destroyed by Mud, Friend's Footprints were printed on the ground and The Enriched Scent Turned Into Muddy Smell.

It Took 2 months for king to prepare all that arrangement and only 10 minutes to ruin all that and then When he left while hanging a bag and he shouted "king, are hum to phakeer admi hai jhola leke chal padenge ji"

Jokes Aside:

Ego is also the same thing it take years to built but a second for someone to destroy, when you spent years and months on building something and it blows in inch of a second then it pains a lot.

In Arrange Marriage it Is Exactly like the same, When Some Elders Spends years of his life in building ego to let his family do as he says including marring the girl of their choice and when his son\daughter Does not follow that stupid ritual and follow up by choice of his\her then that ego shatters and that relationship ends abruptly.

Like some android apps stopped working.

There is very thin line between ego and self respect, The day when people, society will Increase they consciousness till that level where they may distinguish the difference between Ego and self Respect, not also know but accept others decision over theirs then the true revolution shall starts.

Still   Waiting   for   the day...

CHAPTER SIX

DOWRY

"Ayiye Bhai sahab Kuch kaam ki baat karle"

"Come Brother, Lets Talk something Important"

These Sentences sounds familiar to you, Isn't it?

Because you have heard it among your Family, Friends or even Randomly somewhere, because for us its so normal to take Dowry.

Let Me Give You a task to dig deep into Dowry thing and then you will realise the Impact of it our our society, marriage and post Marriage relationship.

Suppose you are a Sales Person and I am giving you a product to sell not to the customer but to the Business Owners it like a B2B market.

What is the first Thing you will say to that Business Owner?

I Heard You wanted a Certain Product?

Here I Have It, Its Fantastic in quality, Durable and Very Great Product Over All.

Now The same Thing happens When We Go to see Bride for our beloved son.

I Heard You wanted a Perfect Son-in-Law, Here It is.

My Son is Very Educated, Fantastic Human Being , Neither He Drink nor any Kind of bad habits So Probably he will last Long (Not sure On Bed).

And Now lets jump back to the Salesperson again,

Our costing for manufacturing this product is So and So rupees, By counting Different Aspects it will Be costing you 5 10 Lakhs Approximately.

Same Story is Repeated In the dowry Also,

My Child Is graduated From XYZ College Delhi and works as a Government Officer and his Monthly salary is Near about 50-90k excluding Bribe.

So My Ask is For 12 Lakhs Cash (For 100 percent Equity of my son), A Four Wheeler Car and Rest Its up to you, what ever you wish to give it to your daughter,

And all The Dream shatters into the little castle of Brides Family.

These Sentence Always brings a sudden heart attack to the bride's Father.

Sometimes these sentences also comes with a lot of tears of happiness or Sorrow but it comes with tear for sure.

Since the Beginning of this Misery Grooms parents are divided into two parts

We will talk about them later but its great how some parents beautifully market their son by reciting their educational background or even their so called quite behaviour, But only God Knows What the reality is.

- Kind 1 Dowry Askers

These Are the most shameless Dowry Askers you will find much often,

They Ask dowry as its their own money or they have the great experience of asking dowry.

They Are mainly the Old Citizens of the Family, or even they might be your relatives. They Are Most probably present in every Family in the Indian Society.

They Ask it Directly Without any Hesitation or without any Shame. You Will always find Something common in these type.

"As you know our son has been Graduated from XYZ College from Delhi and also has Very hefty Annual package, so this marriage is going to cost near about 50 Lakhs."

"We have also Spend millions on his education to make him stand on this Platform of live where he will feed and take care of your daughter."

Every Girl Father Should ask a question to This kind of dowry Asking Uncles.

So do We have to pay the price of 50 Lakhs so that our daughter lives happily and Fed well Into your House?

Are you Fucking Crazy Uncle ji?

Just ask the Annual Package of that Dowry Uncle it will cost something Around 20-30K PER Month or Round figure 3lakhs per annum and they are aking a dowry of 50 lakhs Nearly 16 Times Of their annual wealth.

Have they Lost their Mind?

Its like they need 16 years to earn that money and asking it in one slot.

This Shows the level Of Greediness This Society has for Money, Money AND Money.

- Kind 2 Dowry Askers

Kind 2 Have A unique Marketing Statics, They Wont ask for any Cash, Car nor any Items they will just say,

"What Ever you wish to give it to your daughter we will accept it"

Now the Pressure has turned into the Girl Family,

What we Should Give?

How Much Should We Give?

What if they Didn't Like it?

And Many Such Random obvious Questions.

But Kind 2 Dowry Uncles are Very Sharp and Cunning.

They are Bit Rare to find because due to high Increase in level one type they are rapidly decreasing in Quantity but very Much Of updated Quality.

So If you see someone like this Just Bow them And make sure they realise that they are Slowing going Extinct.

Dowry Is Very Shameful Kind of act.

Indian Society is So well groomed in such a way that in many Places Mindset of people are so broad that they don't ask someone to return their money in public places or in general.

People Just leave By saying "I know him very Well He Will return it When Ever He will Get it."

Some People are even too shy to ask their money back but In the same Locality You will also find an Old Dowry Uncle with 20+ Years of experience in asking dowry. He is one of the favourite Candidate of Sons Father who has well Grown his Child.

But The Problem Doesn't Lies in that Old Uncle but lies inside the Father who Takes this kind of People While going to choose a bride for his son.

Who are They?

Did They ever Supported you Son when He needed?

Does Your Son Even Know Him well?

Do he Knows about the Behaviour of your son or interests?

Its So Sad to see that here in India People Know that dowry is a crime and its wrong in 21 century but still people ask it. Currently no one is able to explain the reason why is it so but let me give it a try.

People In India or A Human Encircle Overall Knows What is Wrong and What Is Right but He Still Try to Do that Act Because Of Two Reasons:

• He is Coward

Now First It Sounded Harsh As Well But Let Me Tell Very Clearly

In My Lifespan of 22 Years I've Met several People Who Want to Raise their Voice against the Bad element or rituals of the society but Couldn't Due to Some Family Pressure or Maybe Some of their personal issues.

I Won't Consider Society Fear Because Society is Nothing to be Feared About its like A Swamp in the Desert, Once You Entered Into it, Then It Will Hold You Forever and then Their Is No escape from Fear.

Society Is Neither to Be Feared nor To be answered It just needs to be Faced.

Wheather You Have Your Answers Figured out or not, Either you are Fearful or fearless it Just need to be Faced.

And In Dowry People Wanted to Raise Their Voice Especially Into Arrange Marriage but They Couldn't,

Youths Of Today are Well Trained and Informed about the Causes and Emotional break through from Dowry But they are not brave enough to Face Their Family who is Standing From the side of Dowry.

On the either side In love Marriage Couples had already faced so much and they fought enough that They stand together in This Battle as well.

Now People Might Say I've Seen People Taking Dowry In Love Marriage?

Dude Let me Explain This Illogical Question,

The Entire Human Encircle Revolves Around I'm Right Sort of thing.

The Only Thing Humans are Afraid to face Is someone is telling him That you are wrong.

So the Same Procedure Follows Here,

When I told You About Dowry In Arrange Marriage Which is Absolutely Common In Today's apart from Love Marriage you Mind got stuck into the face that I've seen People Taking Dowry In Arrange Marriage Which I Totally Agree With The Fact.

When Their Is a Light Their Must be A Darker Shade Before

But Here What are You Doing is,

You Are Taking A Small Quantity of a Matter from A Rare Circle and Comparing it with some Thing that is happening at a totally different level.

So That's Totally Fine I Hope You Got My point.

- You are Getting Advantage From It

One More Valid Reason why people Don't raise their voice against the bad rituals or tradition of the society.

Suppose You Have Got A Job in a Government Office and Your age is Near about 26 and you are just planning to be married (Obviously not Love Marriage) Government Employee are famous for stealing love rather then doing one.

So Now the Only Option Left With You is To Get a Bride through Arrange Marriage. Now You Start In search of her and though its not compulsory that you are Bound to marriage that one damn girl at any cost(As it in Love Marriage), So you Scroll the profiles, confused Between Better Choices or even if you select a Girl you Don't Know her Completely neither you know about her family background, Her Past, Interest Or Anything you Just Chose her By Looking at her Profile.

So Will You Marry Her?

Even if Her Family Didn't Fulfil Your Wish of 10 Lakh Dowry?

Will you raise your voice against Your Family?

"No I Will Only Marry Her"

Do You have enough guts to repeat this sentence in front of your family member?

No Obviously You Won't Or why Would you?

You Have A Government Job,

You are Just 26 Years Old

You Have Many Profiles Still Pending to be Checked

Why Would You Raise Your Voice?

Do You Have Enough Valid Argument To Cross My Perception?

Now As we All know that Every Coin has two sides, Now lets Turn the Situation Up Side Down And watch It from the Female Family side.

Every Father Wants to Marry Her Daughter To the best man In the Town who has A Well settled life and a Good Family for them If such Invitation has been made from the Male side they Will give 10 Lakh Dowry No matter how.

They Will Take Loan, End Up All His saving or They will arrange money no matter from where.

So The Male side will only see 10 Lakh Crediting into their bank account they will totally unaware of the fact that how Other side has arranged it.

So Eventually,

The People who are tying relationship with you Saying I'll keep your daughter safe and healthy are the one who are suppressing daughter's side completely.

In Case you are Reading a book and Still Thinking about asking Dowry Then You should Probably Repeat After Me:
O Lord,
I'm the most Useless Person Ever,
from now I'm Not Able to feed My family so that's why I'm Taking 10Lakh Dowry.
May Your Mercy Fell Upon Me.

CHAPTER SEVEN

VIOLENCE

Did You Know that

Encyclopedia Britannica states that in the early 1800s, most legal systems implicitly accepted wife-beating as a husband's right over his wife. English Common Law dating back to the 16th century, treated as a crime against the community rather than against the individual woman by charging wife beating as a breach of Peace. Wives had the right to seek redress in the form of a Peace Bond from a local Justice for the peace. Procedures were informal and off the record, and no legal guidance specified the standard of proof or degree of violence which would suffice for a conviction.

And Now Lets Talk About India,

According to a National Family and Health Survey in 2005, total lifetime prevalence of domestic violence was 33.5% and 8.5% for sexual violence among women aged 15–49

The 2012 National Crime Record Bureau report of India states a reported crime rate of 46 per 100,000, rape rate of 2 per 100,000, dowry homicide rate of 0.7 per 100,000 and the rate of domestic cruelty by husband or his relatives as 5.9 per 100,000.These reported rates are significantly smaller than the reported intimate partner domestic violence rates in many countries, such as the United States (590 per 100,000) and reported homicide (6.2 per 100,000 globally), crime and rape incidence rates per 100,000 women for most nations tracked by the United Nations.

A 2014 study in The Lancet states, "Whereas an 8.5% prevalence of sexual violence in the country [India] is among the lowest in the world, it is estimated to affect 27.5 million women in India [given India's large population]".Further, the 2006 survey found that 85% of women who suffered sexual violence, in or outside of marriage, never sought help, and only 1% report it to the police.

(All The Data Given Here Are From Wikipedia)

Let Me Repeat a Line

The 2006 survey found that 85% of women who suffered sexual violence, in or outside of marriage, never sought Help.

Domestic Violence In Any Aspect, Region or at any level is a threat to society, But it is also a fact that Arranged Marriages Face A Vital Part among The Crimes that are taking part against women.

In Love Marriage The Chances Of Domestic Violence is Less Because The Partners Understands each other, They Care and they Value their Feelings.

I'm Not saying that People Don't value or understand in Arrange Marriage but it Takes Time for Anyone to Understand Someone Completely and till then its too Far or its too dull for a female to raise a voice, But Its Better Late Then Never.

As We all know that Daughters are More Close to her Father,

And No one can care More About Fathers Then Their Daughters.

So Their are majority of women Who Don't raise their Voice against Domestic Violence because of Her Family.

How Their Family Will React?

How Society Will Judge Her?

How Will She Manage?

The Domestic Violence Affected Daughter Has Seen Her Father Struggling With Money Issue, Smiling Into Her Marriage, Crying While She was Leaving so She Never Thinks Of Complaining An FIR Against The Culprit and ruining a marriage but That Doesn't Mean She Is Weak

That Means That She Has Enough, She is just Giving You Another Chance

Day By Day,

Day By Day

Day by Day

But Not Everyday

CHAPTER EIGHT

LOVE AND LOVE

Lets not go at the extreme ends of the poll,

I've Seen Plenty of Happy Arranged Marriage and Broken Love Marriages.

So Its Not about The Type Of the Marriage Its About Dealing It Further.

A Marriage Is Like A Beautiful Rose,

Many Arrange Marriages have Blossomed Like a Rose and Many Love Marriages Have Dried like A Rose, Yes! Roses also Dry. Some Dry After Few Weeks and some dry within Few days So the Question is not about Rose its about the people Taking Care Of the Rose.

When You Wish to Blossom your rose at Very Best, You can't just Wait for a single person to Make it Happen. Only The Sunlight Is Not Responsible For Blossoming a flower, Gardener also Plays as Important role as Sunlight.

A Gardener Needs to Take care of that little seed and wait until it becomes a bud and still he needs to be patient and wait to convert that little bud into flower and then Happiness Arrives. During the Process In Which A Seed Converts into Rose Both Gardener and Sun Needs to Give A Daily Presence and Share What Ever they have With the rose.

This Is Called a Good Conversation.

To Be in A Happy Marriage, Most Important Thing Is Conversation.

Suppose One Day that Rose Didn't Get a Proper Sunlight or the Other Day The Gardener is absent then Obviously Rose will Dry Soon.

Apart from that Their are Much More Thing which are Required For a Flower to blossom

Fertile Soil, Water, Safety From Stranger and Air

Marriages are Also Like same You Need Trust, Understanding, Freedom and the Most Important Think Safety From Stranger In other Words Stay Away From Extra Marital Affairs.

Extra Marital Affairs are Very Best at ruining marriages.

If you are not sure about that one girl whom you can spend your whole life upon then Don't Marry her Simply

If You are Not Sure about Your Behaviour Regarding External affairs then Please Don't marry, Its not about a single affairs its about The future of two families, Two human beings and much more.

Their is Very Famous True Story

In 2012, bomb disposal expert Taylor Morris was severely injured after the explosion of an improvised bomb in Afghanistan. The explosion took all his limbs and changed the life of the 23-year-old US military soldier forever. While recovering from the injuries in hospital, Taylor was confronted with the painful realization that his limbs had gone. He also had to face the fact that he would be dependent on assistance for the rest of his life. It was an incredibly difficult situation not only for him but also his family and especially his long-term girlfriend Danielle. But instead of ever giving him up, Danielle became Taylor's pillar in life. She helped him recover and took care of him during this incredibly challenging time.

Danielle played an important role in Taylor's quick recovery. She never went away from his side and assisted him greatly when he learned to walk again with his new prosthetic limbs. After Taylor had recovered, he proposed to his beloved girlfriend and they got married. It's a beautiful ending of an incredibly inspiring love story that shows that nothing can ever stand in-between to people who really love each other.

Its Not About the 1000 Reasons we Need to be Apart Its About that One Reason to Stick.

And To stick Forever.

CHAPTER NINE

SETTLEMENTS

Settlement.

A Word That Sounds Defeat for An Egoistic Person, But is It so?

Settlement Is a great word for a person with no ego.

In a Bond of love whether its a marriage or a relationship people need to Settle things down over time or Even Sometime they need to settle Their Emotions, Wishes or even their Feelings Sometimes.

Settlements Simply Don't Mean that You Lost, It Simply Means You Value the Relationship more then Being Right.

Into His Book From Sex to Superconsciousness Osho Tell Us About The Beautiful story About Love and Ego,

There was once an ancient and majestic tree, with branches spreading out towards the sky. When it was in a flowering mood, butterflies of all shapes, colours and sizes danced around it. When it grew blossoms and bore fruit, birds from far lands came and sang in it. The branches, like outstretched hands, blessed all who came and sat in their shade. A small boy used to come and play under it, and the big tree developed an affection for the small boy.

Love between big and small is possible, if the big is not aware that it is big. The tree did not know it was big; only man has that kind of knowledge. The big always has the ego as its prime concern, but for love, nobody is big or small. Love embraces whomsoever comes near.

So the tree developed a love for this small boy who used to come to play near it. Its branches were high, but it bent and bowed them down so that he might pluck its flowers and pick its fruit. Love is ever ready to bow; the ego is never ready to bend. If you approach the ego, its branches will stretch upwards even more; it will stiffen so you cannot reach it so they may sit on the crown somewhere in delhi.

The playful child came, and the tree bowed its branches. The tree was very pleased when the child plucked some flowers; its entire being was filled with the joy of love. Love is always happy when it can give something; the ego is always happy when it can take.

The boy grew. Sometimes he slept on the tree's lap, sometimes he ate its fruit, and sometimes he wore a crown of the tree's flowers and acted like a jungle king. One becomes like a king when the flowers of love are there, but one becomes poor and miserable when the thorns of the ego are present. To see the boy wearing a crown of flowers and dancing about filled the tree with joy. It nodded in love; it sang in the breeze. The boy grew even more. He began to climb the tree to swing on its branches. The tree felt very happy when the boy rested on its branches. Love is happy when it gives comfort to someone; the ego is only happy when it gives discomfort.

With the passage of time the burden of other duties came to the boy. Ambition grew; he had exams to pass; he had friends to chat with and to wander about with, so he did not come often. But the tree waited anxiously for him to come. It called from its soul, "Come. Come. I am waiting for you." Love waits day and night. And the tree waited. The tree felt sad when the boy did not come. Love is sad when it cannot share; love is sad when it cannot give. Love is grateful when it can share. When it can surrender, totally, love is the happiest.

As he grew, the boy came less and less to the tree. The man who becomes big, whose ambitions grow, finds less and less time for love. The boy was now engrossed in worldly affairs.

One day, while he was passing by, the tree said to him, "I wait for you but you do not come. I expect you daily."

The boy said, "What do you have? Why should I come to you? Have you any money? I am looking for money." The ego is always motivated. Only if there is some purpose to be served will the ego come. But love is motiveless. Love is its own reward.

The startled tree said, "You will come only if I give something?" That which withholds is not love. The ego amasses, but love gives unconditionally. "We don't have that sickness, and we are joyful," the tree said. "Flowers bloom on us. Many fruits grow on us. We give soothing shade. We dance in the breeze, and sing songs. Innocent birds hop on our branches and chirp even though we don't have any money. The day we get involved with money, we will have to go to the temples like you weak men do, to learn how to obtain peace, to learn how to find love. No, we do not have any need for money."

The boy said, "Then why should I come to you? I will go where there is money. I need money." The ego asks for money because it needs power.
The tree thought for a while and said, "Don't go anywhere else, my dear. Pick my fruit and sell it. You will get money that way."

The boy brightened immediately. He climbed up and picked all the tree's fruit; even the unripe ones were shaken down. The tree felt happy, even though some twigs and branches were broken, even though some of its leaves had fallen to the ground. Getting broken also makes love happy, but even after getting, the ego is not happy. The ego always desires more. The tree didn't notice that the boy hadn't even once looked back to thank him. It had had its thanks when the boy accepted the offer to pick and sell its fruit.

The boy did not come back for a long time. Now he had money and he was busy making more money from that money. He had forgotten all about the tree. Years passed. The tree was sad. It yearned for the boy's return – like a mother whose breasts are filled with milk but whose son is lost. Her whole being craves for her son; she searches madly for her son so he can come to lighten her. Such was the inner cry of that tree. Its entire being was in agony. After many years, now an adult, the boy came to the tree.

The tree said, "Come, my boy. Come embrace me."

The man said, "Stop that sentimentality. That was a childhood thing. I am not a child any more." The ego sees love as madness, as a childish fantasy.

But the tree invited him: "Come, swing on my branches. Come dance. Come play with me."

The man said, "Stop all this useless talk! I need to build a house. Can you give me a house?"

The tree exclaimed: "A house! I am without a house." Only men live in houses. Nobody else lives in a house but man. And do you notice his condition after his confinement among four walls? The bigger his buildings, the smaller man becomes. "We do not stay in houses, but you can cut and take away my branches – and then you may be able to build a house."

Without wasting any time, the man brought an axe and severed all the branches of the tree. Now the tree was just a bare trunk. But love cares not for such things – even if its limbs are severed for the loved one. Love is giving; love is ever ready to give.

The man didn't even bother to thank the tree. He built his house. And the days flew into years.

The trunk waited and waited. It wanted to call for him, but it had neither branches nor leaves to give it strength. The wind blew by, but it couldn't even manage to give the wind a message. And still its soul resounded with one prayer only: "Come. Come, my dear. Come." But nothing happened.

Time passed and the man had now become old. Once he was passing by and he came and stood by the tree.

The tree asked, "What else can I do for you? You have come after a very, very long time."

The old man said, "What else can you do for me? I want to go to distant lands to earn more money. I need a boat, to travel."

Cheerfully, the tree said, "But that's no problem, my love. Cut my trunk, and make a boat from it. I would be so very happy if I could help you go to faraway lands to earn money. But, please remember, I will always be awaiting your return."

The man brought a saw, cut down the trunk, made a boat and sailed away.

Now the tree is a small stump. And it waits for its loved one to return. It waits and it waits and it waits. The man will never return; the ego only goes where there is something to gain and now the tree has nothing, absolutely nothing to offer. The ego does not go where there is nothing to gain.

The ego is an eternal beggar, in a continuous state of demand, and love is charity. Love is a king, an emperor! Is there any greater king than love?

I was resting near that stump one night. It whispered to me, "That friend of mine has not come back yet. I am very worried in case he might have drowned, or in case he might be lost. He may be lost in one of those faraway countries. He might not even be alive any more. How I wish for news of him! As I near the end of my life, I would be satisfied with some news of him at least. Then I could die happily. But he would not come even if I could call him. I have nothing left to give and he only understands the language of taking."

The Tree Settled To Every Aspect of the Kid and Hence Enjoyed the purest form of love but The Man Always uses that Settlement to benefit Himself, That was Not Love

You Need to See and Enjoy The Purest Form of love that can be achieved by Entire Human Race. It Can be of Parents-Son, Lovers, Married, Or Even If you have Your Pet. Love Them Without Ego. Get Ready For Every Possible way To be Get Settled. If You Think Nothing Is Going as Your Way or as You Thought about Your Relationship Just Remember

Wait, Sort and Live

CHAPTER TEN

YES TO LOVE

So now I've Completed My first Book I Haven't Thought of The Title yet, Hence You are reading it That Seems that I've Provided a Suitable Title and Finally My Book has Been Published.

And Now This Book is Something Which I'll Keep it Save Because Now i have my Feelings Attached to it Isn't It?

Obviously I'll Keep It Very Safe Take Care of it and Will Protect it From Any Particle That Tries To harm it.

So It took me Nearly 4 Months To Write this book AND NOW I'M Very Much Attached to it.

I don't Understand a simple Question If I am Attached to My First Book Just in 4 Months, Why People are Not Attached To Someone they have been Living Since Years?

Married Couples Are Fighting,

Relationships Of the People are Breaking as if Nothing

Parents and Their Children are Not In a Good Relationship

Why This All is Happening?

Because We Have Forgotten The Love

Now In this Book I'M Not going to Say What Is love but Maybe If She Asks For a Second book I Might Consider.

Arrange Marriages Are something needs to be seen closely because marriages are not something For seven lives its Just About one Life, This Life

Next 6 Nobody Will See Neither You Nor me.

So Choose A Partner that Makes You Happy In this Birth. Leave All Other 6